Glanum

From Salluvian oppidum to Roman city

by Anne Roth Congès, *chargée de recherches*
at the *Centre National de la Recherche Scientifique*

The ruins of the ancient city of Glanum in Provence are now a popular destination on the tourist route that leads from Avignon to Arles, passing Les Baux and the abbey of Montmajour. Until the beginning of the 20th century, however, only two well preserved monuments, a mausoleum and an arch, known as "Les Antiques", signalled Glanum's location and its past glory. Situated at the meeting point of the wild Alpilles hills and the gentle plain, the walls of this Greek and Gallo-Roman city were uncovered by painstaking archaeological work. Thanks to the research of archaeologists Pierre de Brun and Henri Rolland, Glanum, which is scarcely mentioned by classical authors, has now been given a posthumous future and is today one of the best-known and most spectacular classical sites in France. In this arid landscape, the healing

waters of a spring gave rise to a Celto-Ligurian civilization, which exceptionally at Glanum, was able to accept and profit from the cultural fashions of the Hellenistic Mediterranean world long before it had to conform to Roman directives.

"Les Antíques"
inspired this
imaginary
composition by
Hubert Robert
in 1786: Glanum's
mausoleum (left)
and arch (right)
are depicted with
the triumphal
arch (foreground)
and the wall
of the theatre
(background)
in Orange.
(Oil, Paris, Musée
du Louvre).

Iron Age Sanctuary of the Salluvii

6th-2nd centuries BC

All the objects depicted are in the "Hôtel de Sade", unless otherwise stated.

Left-hand page
The spring
is harnessed in the building in the foreground, under the arch.

Altar
(h.: 1.57m; w.: 0.77m) dedicated to the god Glanis and the Glanic mother goddesses by a veteran of the 21st Legion, stationed on the Rhine (1st century AD).

Situated between the Lubéron and the Mediterranean Sea, near the Rhône delta, the Alpilles hills separate the stony steppe of the Crau to the south from the gentler plain of the Durance to the north. There are only a few passes through the steep, though not very high Alpilles, such as the narrow gorge of Notre-Dame-de-Laval, which today connects Saint-Rémy-de-Provence with Maussane. At its northern end a permanent spring has been occupied since Neolithic times and was surrounded by an adjoining Salluvian ◆ settlement, Glanum, during the Iron Age (6th-2nd century BC).

Among the offerings thrown into the basin of the spring and the rocky cave overlookings the sanctuary are painted and engraved stone steles, pottery and coins. They demonstrate the religious nature of the site from its origin. A Celtic god, Glanis, and his beneficent companions, the "Glanic Mothers", were believed to inhabit these crystalline healing waters.

Three-horned bull.
This bronze figurine (6cm tall) represents a Celtic deity (Tarvos Trigaranos?) often linked to sacred springs.

◆**Salluvii:**
A Gallic people of Provence.

A Vast Oppidum Surrounded by a Rampart

Aerial view of Glanum looking north, tracing the line of the Iron Age ramparts (M.Gazenbeek)

Between the 6th and 2nd centuries BC, a first drystone rampart (yellow tracing) protected the small Notre-Dame valley and the adjacent heights, such as the natural fortress of Mont Gaussier. Together with the cross-wall blocking the entry to the gorge, the rampart encircled the road over the Alpilles for a stretch of 300 metres and enclosed some 20 hectares by following the crest of the hills. As a result the oppidum♦ of Glanum differs from most contemporary indigenous sites, which were entirely constructed on heights.

With the expansion of the city to the north and east beyond its fortification, at the end of the 2nd or the beginning of the 1st century BC, this rampart was complemented by a new wall (red tracing) that doubled the enclosed surface. It incorporated the small Saint-Clerg Valley, and still followed as far as possible the crest of the hills. Some remains of towers have been found. This second fortification, like many others in the lower Rhône valley, might be related to the Germanic invasions (Teutons and Ambrons). They were defeated by the Roman general Marius near Aix-en-Provence in 102 BC after three years of campaigning, military preparations and associated civil engineering. This included the construction of a canal from Arles to the sea in order to facilitate communication and commerce – the *Fossae Marianae* which give their name to Fos-sur-Mer.

♦*Oppidum:* A term used for fortified indigenous settlements, often hilltop sites.

These two ramparts have been almost entirely dismantled and have only recently been rediscovered by archaeological field surveys.

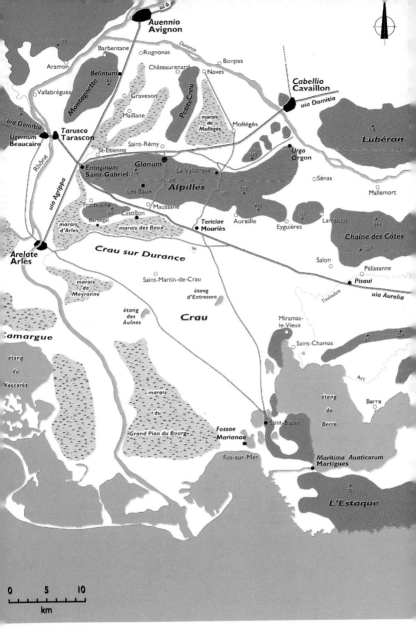

Glanum in the lower Rhône valley, Provence.

Glanum is located slightly away from the major crossroads at Ernaginum, west of the Alpilles, where the *via Agrippa*, which follows the Rhône, meets the main roads that connect Italy with Spain: the *via Aurelia* along the coast and the *via Domitia* through the Alps. Glanum is situated near the latter on a connecting road to the *via Aurelia*.

heights

marshes

ancient roads

• ancient settlements

○ modern settlements

Glanic nobleman sitting cross-legged on a base decorated with acroteria (0.8m tall).
He is clothed in a fine tunic above his thighs, leaving his genitals naked, and wears a cape fastened over his breast, a torque (Gallic necklace), as well as a bracelet around his left biceps. Comparable representations of this type, with or without weapons and often decapitated are known from other Salluvian sites: Roquepertuse, Entremont, Constantine, La Cloche, etc.

Limestone lintel (l.: 2.45m; h.: 0.4m; w.: 0.51m) crowned by leaf and dart on both sides, with cavities to receive human skulls.

Indigenous tomb from the Thor Blanc district. The stele is complete, but not inscribed. The caisson contained a funerary urn, four vases and a bronze cup (2nd half of the 1st century BC).

Upper part of a stele from the district of La Galine with inscription in Gallic language but in Greek characters: OURITTA/ KOCHLO/ UCKONI/OC. (VrItaccos, son of Elusku). End of 2nd-beginning 1st century BC.

Classical historians and geographers recognised two supposedly indigenous populations in southeast Gaul: the Ligurians inhabited the coast from Genoa to the Rhône and presumably also the Hérault, while the Iberians occupied the coast to the west. They also knew that Celtic people had been "assimilated" into the native populations giving rise to so-called Celto-Ligurian and Celto-Iberian peoples. Archaeological research can verify these assertions without revealing many details. We merely know the date and the modes of the Celtic implantation, starting in the First Iron Age at the latest (7th-5th centuries BC), followed by more intense Celtic immigration during the Second Iron Age (4th-1st centuries BC), with varying intensity in different regions. The Glanices belonged to a confederation of tribes, the Salluvii, inhabiting the area from the Mediterranean coast to the Lubéron, and from the Rhône to an unknown border in the East, maybe as far east as Antibes.

Personal names are of Celtic origin: Vrittakos, Elusku, Bimmos, Litumaros, Sigotoutiorix, Esken-gorvos, Epo[redorix], etc. So are the names of gods, such as Glanis and his com-panions, the "Glanic Mothers", as well as other mother goddesses (e.g. Rokloisiai, "those who listen"), Sucellus and Epona. Other Gallic divinities are concealed under Greco-Roman names, such as Apollo, Mercury and Fortuna. The Gallic language appears on numerous epitaphs, dedications and honorary inscriptions in Glanum, as well as throughout the lower Rhône valley. The habit of exhibiting the skulls of enemies at the city gates and in houses is Celtic in origin as are statues sitting cross-legged. These probably represent high dignitaries, sometimes depicted with weapons. Even the culinary pottery recovered on the site reveals a clear preference for continental-style boiled meat cooked in cooking pots, rather than Mediterranean-style fried meat.

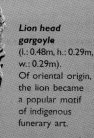

Lion head gargoyle (l.: 0.48m, h.: 0.29m, w.: 0.29m). Of oriental origin, the lion became a popular motif of indigenous funerary art.

The Golden Age and the Roman Conquest

2nd-early 1st century BC

Head of a man and head of Apollo crowned with laurel. Despite the capital's Mediterranean style, Apollo is also considered to be the principal god of the Gauls.

The Celtic character of Glanum is obvious. However, the proximity of the Greek city of Marseilles (founded by the Phocaeans in 600 BC) and an easy access to the sea encouraged contacts between the Rhône delta and Mediterranean civilisations. The great indigenous aristocratic and warrior families were open to Hellenistic contributions and this gave rise to a new cultural identity, the so-called Gallo-Greek culture, of which Glanum is the finest example known to us. But increasing tension with Marseilles incited the Greeks to ask Rome for help. The Salluvii were defeated by the Roman consul Marcus Fulvius Flaccus in 125 BC, and again by Gaius Sextius Calvinus in the following year, who also founded *Aquae Sextiae* (Aix-en-Provence) in 122 BC. Glanum's monuments were destroyed, but far from admitting defeat, the local dignitaries started a remarkable building boom, covering Glanum's narrow valleys with even more impressive houses and public monuments. At the peak of its prosperity, principally based on the prestige of the healing sanctuary, the city issued silver coins in its own name ("Glanikon").

This Golden Age was brought to an end by a final revolt of the Salluvii in 90 BC, which was immediately subdued by the Roman consul Caecilius. Most of Glanum's monuments were demolished and the city took a long time to recover from its ruined state. Relatively modest houses replaced the beautiful public buildings at the heart of Glanum. The first half of the 1st century BC was a difficult period for the whole of *Provincia* (southern Gaul), in particular Pompey's bloody expedition in 77 BC and the regime of the vicious praetor Fonteius. Even though the Salluvii had finally been subjugated, the rebellions of neighbouring peoples brought violent responses from Rome.

Silver *tetrobolon* | 11 **minted in the name of the *Glanikai* (190g).** The crowned head perhaps represents one of the Glanic mother goddesses. The bull, surrounded by a reed or ear of corn symbolises the sacred spring and fertility (end of 2nd century BC, Paris, BnF).

Statue of the imprisoned Gaul (h.: 1.10m, w.: 0.65m) from the triumphal fountain in the forum.

A City in Narbonensis

1st century BC-3rd century AD

The curia
was the council
chamber in
Roman times;
its semi-circular
apse contained
a statue of
the emperor.

In 49 BC Gaius Julius Caesar seized Marseilles and on its confiscated territory he founded the colony of Arles *(Arelate)* in 45 BC. Subsequently people in *Provincia* were faced with mayhem, especially during the civil wars, when Roman generals (Octavian, Mark Antony, Lepidus), fighting for absolute power, repeatedly confiscated and redistributed land to veteran soldiers. This was followed by a vast administrative reorganisation that defined the status of cities. Whereas many, like Glanum, were granted Latin rights as *oppidum Latinum*, only a few were elevated to the more prestigious rank of colony. This latter defined the status of a city which was founded by Rome in conquered territory, often in order to accommodate demobilised soldiers who were each given a land allotment. When Octavian became the emperor Augustus in 27 BC, he created the province of Narbonensis, which was administered by the Senate from 22 BC onwards.

Map of cities in southeast Gaul at the beginning of the Empire

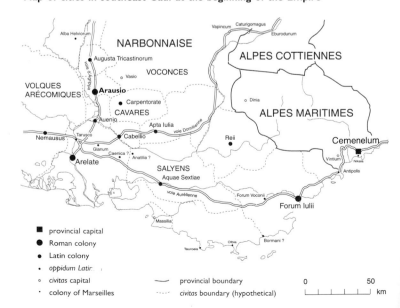

The status of *oppidum Latinum* allowed Glanum's aristocracy to acquire the prestigious Roman citizenship by serving as local magistrates, giving them the full civic and political rights of Rome. Some — e. g. the Iulii, builders of the mausoleum at the entrance of Glanum — had received the rights already for long military service, or through the personal favour of high-ranking Roman statesmen or generals. Besides their political and administrative role in the city, these elites actively contributed to embellishing the city, conforming to patterns imposed by Rome. Among the obligatory urban components were the forum, temples, public baths and buildings for entertainment. These were places where the population could gather and imperial ideology was communicated, by the magnificence of the decor, the symbolism of images and the rituals of the imperial cult.

Marble portraits of imperial princesses (h.: 22.5cm and 26.5cm) found near the twin temples (end of 1st century BC).

Glanum probably received the title of Latin colony, perhaps as early as the Augustan period. Its people had a rather peaceful life under the Empire, though less dazzling than in the Salluvian past, and more modest than the neighbouring colonies of Arles, Avignon and Cavaillon. The increasing importance of the official cult of the emperor and his family overshadowed Glanum's traditional cult of the healing spring at the origin of the city's prosperity. The decline of this sanctuary could not be counterbalanced by any other economic success, since Glanum was not directly on a major line of communication (the *via Domita*). In the late 2nd and early 3rd century AD Glanum's people were still

Dedication of the inhabitants of Glanum to the emperor Caracalla in AD 198, probably associated with a statue on the forum.

The Dam
and the Western Aqueduct

In the 19th century, a modern dam was constructed in the same location as the Roman one.

Reconstruction of the Roman dam and the subsequent western aqueduct (J.-L. Paillet).

A survey of the cuts on the rocky flanks of the narrow Peyrous valley, west of Glanum, allows a graphic reproduction of the dam, which collected the water of the Alpilles, and of the aqueduct, which brought it into the city. From the convex construction of the dam's wall, it becomes clear that this is the oldest known arch-dam (c. end of the 1st century BC?). The aqueduct was supported by arcades and among the recipients of its water was the triumphal fountain in the forum.

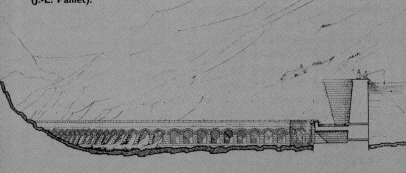

dynamic enough to enrich the forum and baths with marble, and many dedications (probably accompanying statues that did not survive) were put up to honour the imperial household.

However Glanum did not survive the Alemannic invasions in AD 260, and its inhabitants abandoned the site and founded a new settlement along the road. In the Merovingian age this belonged to the Abbey of Saint-Rémy, Reims.

Mont Gaussier (307m).
This natural bulwark, protected on all sites by steep cliffs, was the acropolis of the Salluvian oppidum and became a fortress again from the 11th to the 13th centuries AD.

Early Christian and Medieval Occupation

In the 4th and 5th centuries AD Glanum became a vast stone quarry and most of its monuments were dismantled. The sewage system was no longer maintained and the area degraded so that a thick layer of alluvium covered the site. However, some buildings were constructed during the 5th and 6th centuries AD around the spring. In the 10th century, medieval records mention the domain of Fretus in this area, and Mont Gaussier *(castellum Iaucerii)* was fortified in the 11th century AD by a family related to the first Counts of Provence. Two centuries later a *castrum Gaucerio* was recorded, suggesting a possible settlement around the castle. Nothing is mentioned in the records after AD 1240.

View of "Les Antiques"
of St Remy from
the west side,
by Meunier (1792?),
pen and watercolour
(Paris, BnF).

The Rediscovery of the Ancient City

From the 16th century, "Les Antiques" were known to scholars and travellers. King Charles IX made a visit in 1564 and restored the surroundings. Numerous finds of sculptures, inscriptions, coins, etc. were recorded during the 17th and 18th centuries and in the 19th century the Marquis of Lagoy explored the small valleys of Notre-Dame and Saint-Clerg. Jules Formigé, Historic Monuments architect, initiated the first systematic excavations as late as 1921. Pierre de Brun supervised them for twenty years, excavating the area of the basilica, the houses of the northern quarter and the public baths. At the same time, from 1928 to 1933, Henri Rolland (1887-1970) excavated the Iron Age sanctuary to the south.

Left-hand page **Excavations by Pierre de Brun** around the Baths' street (late 1930s).

♦Hellenistic (period): *From the death of Alexander the Great to the time of Augustus (4th-1st centuries BC).*

Henri Rolland was director of the excavations from 1942 to 1969 which progressed from north to south, i.e. from the forum to the sanctuary in the gorge. Every year the discoveries became more spectacular and deep excavations revealed the remains of much earlier phases of the city. We owe this scholar the basis of our understanding of the site, the systematic publications, the classifications, the surveys, as well as the public exhibition of the many finds in the "Hôtel de Sade" in Saint-Rémy-de-Provence.

Pierre de Brun (left, in the 1920s) and **Henri Rolland** (right, 1951) with the portrait of an imperial princess. Photomontage by Jean-Claude Fontan.

Excavations of the monumental fountain under the forum in 1989. One can distinguish the architecture slabs and fragments of the imperial dedications.

The excavations have continued since 1982, though increasingly the excavators have been involved in conserving the site. A monumental well of the Hellenistic♦ period has been discovered, Glanum's southern district re-examined and the gate of the rampart and the foundations of a temple investigated. Field surveys have allowed the study of various aspects of the infrastructure, such as the dam, two aqueducts, and the Iron Age ramparts.

The Visit

"Les Antiques"

The mausoleum and the arch, which mark the northern entrance to the city, are in an exceptional state of preservation. They were spared by the entrepreneurs of late Antiquity who dismantled Glanum and subsequent centuries have cared for both monuments. Today, however, their sculptures are threatened by atmospheric pollution.

The Mausoleum

The mausoleum, a monumental tomb, is situated immediately outside the north entrance to the city. This is the best location for a necropolis. One has to imagine rows of funerary monuments on both sides of the road, although they would certainly have been of more modest dimensions than the surviving mausoleum. On the architrave◆ facing the road, there is an inscribed dedication which tells us that "Sextus, Lucius and Marcus Iulius, sons of Gaius, [offered this tomb] to their parents" (SEX. L. M. IVLIEI. C. F. PARENTIBVS. SVEIS).

This mausoleum was built by three brothers, whose name was Iulius (also the name of Julius Caesar's family), for their father, mother and probably for their eldest brother too. It is likely that the two toga-wearing statues in the *tholos* at the top are the father and the eldest

The mausoleum, cross-section and details by J. Formigé, pen and wash, 1915 (Paris, MAP).

brother; the mother is not represented, which was normal at that time. It was Roman custom that the first son carried the forename of his father; but the name Gaius does not appear among the three signatory brothers who made this dedication, implying that he had died previously.
There is a very persistent tradition, which ignores comparable examples and

◆*Architrave:*
Horizontal element which rests on columns or on top of a wall.

interprets this monument not as the tomb of a native, Romanised family, though this fact is well attested, but as a cenotaph, i.e. a monument of merely honorary character without burial dedicated to rather "distant" parents. Gaius and Lucius are identified as the emperor Augustus' grandchildren, who died in AD 4 and 2 respectively. But this high-status attribution cannot be sustained. The architectural and artistic characteristics provide a much earlier dating – the 30s BC – than could have been related to the "Princes of the Youth". The missing urns containing the ashes of the deceased, set in the hollow base of the monument's plinth, can be explained by tomb robbers in the past.

Even without this legendary attribution, the Glanum mausoleum is an exceptional testimony to the pride and the social rank of the Iulii, members of the indigenous elite. For their allegiance and for services rendered, notably in the Gallic War, they received Roman citizenship and deserved to carry the name of one of the most prestigious families in Rome. The structure and decor of the mausoleum reveal the origin of this honour.

| 23

◆**Corinthian order:**
Architectural system characterised by capitals with plant motifs.

◆**Archivolt:**
Semi-circular band of moulding on the face of an arch.

◆**Acanthus:**
Plant with large leaves, which was used as a model for the plant motifs in the Corinthian order.

The tholos

The top level is a circular *tholos* (dome) in the Corinthian order◆, sheltering the effigies of two male *togati*, whose heads were replaced in the 18th century. The frieze is decorated by ornamental foliage. The conical roof is covered with scales, common in funeral art, though the ridge acroterion, perhaps a pine-cone, is missing.

The tetrapylon

The second level consists of an arch with four bays in the Corinthian order *(tetrapylon)*. Its symbolism is unmistakably triumphal, but the decor is funerary in origin. The archivolts◆ are decorated with acanthus◆ leaves, symbols of perpetual rebirth, and a Gorgon's head, the protector of the tomb, adorns the keystone. The epitaph is engraved on the architrave on the north side. On the frieze, Tritons carry the solar disc above the ocean, keeping it away from marine monsters, except on the north side where the sun does not appear.

The base

The lower storey rests on a square podium and has pilasters at each corner. Hanging between them are garlands with theatre masks on top, supported by three naked cupids.

The bas-relief panels below are evocative and depict, in a mythical fashion, various heroic aspects of the life of the deceased.

The north panel, below the inscription, depicts the inextricable mêlée of a cavalry battle.

The sculptor knew how to vary the attitudes of the riders, reproduce the excitement of the horses and confer vigour and strength to the whole scene.

He has even taken the liberty of encroaching on the pilasters, two blocks of which have been replaced in the bottom right-hand corner.

In the centre of the east panel

an infantryman unseats an Amazon – a symbolic allusion – locating the battle in the East and thus perhaps evoking the victory of Caesar at Pharnace in 47 BC. Behind the soldier, to the left, a winged Victory carrying a trophy protects him. In the top left-hand corner there is a scene from the hero's distant home: from left to right, two *togati* and a woman listen to a small winged character "Fame" reading the story of the battle from a scroll. The bearded man in the centre is probably the father of the hero, the woman certainly his mother, and the man to the left, who seems to be younger, could be his brother.

The south panel depicts a boar-hunting scene in a forest, symbolised by two dead trees. The animal, emerging from the bottom right-hand side, is attacked by two riders with spears, while two more men, armed with lances, also await it. In the centre, a naked injured man dies in the arms of a companion. Though some mythological tales, such as the

hunting of the Calydonian boar and the death of the Niobides inspired these scenes, the artist adapted them to represent the lives and leisure of the Iulii from Glanum.

The west panel again shows a well-known mythological theme: the fight between the Greeks and Trojans over the remains of Patrocles, who is lying naked on the floor, for the possession of his weapons. Again, this could be a reference to a real event in the history of the family, maybe the death of the eldest son in the course of a battle. The helmets of the soldiers offer a remarkable variety of crests.

The arch,
west side *(above)*,
reconstruction
of the upper part
by J. Bruchet
(centre) and view
by Jean Formigé,
pen and water-
colour, 1915
(Paris, MAP).

The Arch

The arch is less well preserved than the mausoleum. One can reconstruct the top third of the arch above the capitals of the columns with an entablature♦, an attic storey♦, and a pediment (ornamental façade) with dedication. Dating towards the end of Augustus' reign (who died in AD 14), the arch is a symbol of Glanum's municipal dignity and might testify to the status of Latin colony, which the city probably received in this period.

The arch is situated on the invisible boundary that surrounded the city and separated it from its territory: the *pomerium*. This line follows the course of the dismantled rampart which was not considered to be worth rebuilding under the *pax Romana* (Roman Peace). The gate had an important symbolic and legal role that could hardly have escaped a traveller approaching the city: as he left the countryside and the necropolis behind him, he entered a civilised, urban world, a centre of Romanness, subject to orders from Rome and the Emperor.

In fact, the sculptures eloquently tell the story, exalting the triumph of the victor and the civilising mission of the city. On the right panel, a woman sitting on a pile of weapons, next to a chained warrior seen from

☐ reconstructed

0   10 m

◆Entablature:
The three layers overhanging a wall or colonnade that supports a structure (from top to bottom: cornice, frieze, architrave).

◆Attic:
Top storey of a monument above the entablature.

◆Impost:
Projecting slab of masonry between a wall (or a pillar) and a vault (or an arch).

behind, represents defeated Gaul. The left panel shows another prisoner in front of a trophy; on his shoulder is the hand of a character of small stature, with the Gallic coat draped in the Roman fashion. Perhaps he is the son of a warrior, or a Romanised native, who acquired the new culture and denounced the dream of independence and the consequences of rebellion. On the other side there are two pairs of prisoners framing the door elucidating the fate reserved for barbarism. Under the arch are remarkable hexagonal panels with a floral decor bordered by plant motifs. Underneath, musical instruments and knives, probably related to sacrificial rites, enliven the frieze of the imposts◆.

Details of the vault with panels.

From "Les Antiques" to the Excavations

South of "Les Antiques", heading to the entrance of the excavations, one is already in the ancient city of Glanum. Here the remains are either completely destroyed or have not yet been excavated. The hills in the distance show the approximate course of the rampart at its largest extent, around 100 BC.

On the right before going into the entrance hall, there is an **early Christian limestone quarry,** Glanum's major resource for building work and probably for export. On either side of the entrance to the hall are a Corinthian capital and a fragment of ornamental foliage engraved in limestone.

Besides a bookstore and an audio-visual auditorium, **the entrance hall** houses an introduction to the excavations. Various artefacts are exhibited, including copies of sculptures and paintings, everyday objects, documentary panels and two hypothetical models of the city's centre in the 2nd century BC (Hellenistic period) and the 2nd century AD (Roman period).

Overview of the Excavations

Three Major Districts

Leaving the entrance hall, the visitor can see across the whole two-hectare excavation site. Most of the remains on the hills were destroyed, but the remains survived in the narrow valley, which was protected for centuries under layers of sediment. Panel [1] contains a plan of the excavations. From here it is possible to see the entire site and to distinguish three urban areas: the residential district, the monumental city centre and the valley of the sacred spring.

The residential district is on the left and can be identified by its courtyard houses and the public baths at the back.
In the middle, there is the monumental city centre with two obvious buildings: opposite the visitor there is the *curia* with its semi-circular apse — the assembly place of the local senate [38]; to the right, three columns and part of a (restored) frieze mark the site of a temple [29]. The Roman forum occupied the space between the two. In the background a semi-circular lawn marks the presumed site of the theatre [26]. Further to the right, south of the monumental city centre, where the valley narrows to a small gorge, is the sacred spring, which is the *raison d'être* of Glanum. The suggested itinerary takes the visitor to the narrow valley by following the path to the right.

(The superior numbers refer to the plan, indicating observation points and monuments).

A Residential district (p. 58)
B Monumental city centre (p. 44)
C Valley of the sacred spring (p. 36)

Beyond the valley of the sacred spring (foreground)
and "Les Antiques" (top right corner)
the view extends to Saint-Rémy-de-Provence
and the hills between Glanum and the Rhône.

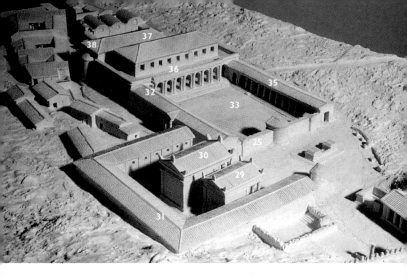

Model
of the Roman
forum, looking
north-east.

**Marble statue
of a young prince**
(h.: 81cm),
found with
the heads of two
princesses near
the twin temple.

The Gallo-Roman Monumental Centre

The next panel [2] provides a plan
of the Gallo-Roman city centre.
Opposite, on the forum square
(1st-3rd centuries AD), the
population assembled for market
days, financial business and liturgies
of the civic cults. The outline
of the forum follows the line
of the present metal fence that
surrounds the excavations.

One has to imagine a
paved plaza [33], with
porticos on either
side [32, 35], and
colonnades
opening onto
it. To the
left, there
are the
remains of
the civil and
judicial
basilica [36]:
the grand hall
(47 x 24
metres) was
supported by
24 sturdy
columns of
which only

the foundations remain (square
masonry blocks, previously
covered by earth). The façade has
completely disappeared, but the
lateral walls and the huge wall at
the bottom made from small
stones have survived. Steps at
the front led to the ground floor,
which should be placed a little
above the top of the columns'
foundations; an ambulatory with a
gallery surrounded the central
nave. At the rear of the basilica
to the left is the *curia* [38], with its
apse, which was adorned by the
emperor's statue, and at the
centre a square room [37], which
served both as courthouse and as
shrine for the imperial cult. In the
2nd century AD a monumental
enclosure with semi-circular
exedra [25] enclosed the forum to
the south.

The original plan of the forum
extended to the south-west and
incorporated two Corinthian
temples [29, 30]. These "twin
temples" (of different dimensions)
were dedicated to the cult of the
emperor and his family. Having
been built in the first years of
Augustus' reign (c. 20-10 BC),
they are clearly earlier than the
basilica and belong to a previous
phase of the forum. The temples
are surrounded on three sides by

The small twin temple (with part of the façade reconstructed). In the foreground the remains of the *peribolos* of the twin temples.

Bottom left
Detail of a cornice of the *peribolos* (end of 1st century BC). In the early years of the Empire a group of local sculptors translated Greco-Roman art forms into rustic, but strong and vigorous images.

a tiered *peribolos*♦ 31, whose northern podium, built in large stones and filled up with small quarry stones, can be seen to the right.

From there the visitor can go up on the right towards the lookout points, or alternatively follow the edge of the valley. Standing behind the "twin temples" 3, one can see the larger temple 30 built along the axis of their courtyard. It has been completely dismantled and only the large stone block foundations – themselves

recycled from 2nd century BC monuments – remain. The smaller temple 29 is squeezed into the available space to the right. The base of its podium, decorated with a frieze, has been preserved, and above, a part of the façade has been restored. It includes a podium, three columns and the corner of the entablature and frieze – a close reproduction of the typical Corinthian decor (capitals, cornices, and acroterion) based on the many fragments found in the excavations.

♦Peribolos:
An enclosed area around a temple often delimited by porticos.

Acroterion from the roof of the large twin temple (end of 1st century BC).

The Belvederes

From behind the twin temples [3], the visitor who does not object to a steep ascent can climb up towards the two viewpoints on the hill. The Pierre de Brun Belvedere [4] overlooks the monumental city centre. An enamel table shows the archaeological remains and illustrates the scale of the twin temples. Further up, the Henri Rolland Belvedere [5] offers a panoramic view of the site and the landscape. Looking north, there is, to the left (west), the Rhône Valley, the Languedoc and the Cévennes, and straight ahead (north) the valley of the Durance, the Comtat plain and the Préalpes. In this land, divided between arid hills and swampy plains, the control of water, whether by irrigation or drainage, is a constant necessity. Agriculture on the hills and in the narrow valleys sustained the people from Glanum in the Iron Age. In Roman times the heavy soils of the plains were put to agricultural use by a network of drainage canals.

From there, a path leads to a deep rocky cavity [6], the rock sanctuary and home of the infernal divinities since prehistoric times. A flight of stairs connects it to its counterpart, the spring sanctuary in the valley [10]. In the first Iron Age, stone stelae with hollow recesses, sometimes painted and engraved, were associated with this cult.

At the point where the two itineraries meet again [7], the natural contraction of this small Alpilles valley was reinforced by a powerful dry-stone rampart [15] dating from the first Iron Age (6th-3rd centuries BC). Walls, 16 metres thick, protected the early *oppidum* that occupied the narrow valley and the surrounding slopes up to Mont Gaussier (one can recognise the remains of buildings cut into the rocky walls).

Left-hand page
The Gallo-Roman monumental city centre, looking north-east. In the foreground to the right the reconstructed corner of the small twin temple. Behind lies the forum square and the basilica, which can be recognised by the foundations of the columns (square masonry blocks).

In the background the tall walls of the curia and the tribunal, with its apse to the left *(photo below).*

The valley of the spring looking east, with labels 13 and 12.

The Valley of the Sacred Spring

The Wine Smokehouse

The valley
of the spring
looking east.
To the left the
sacred spring
and on either side
the Hercules and
Valetudo temples.
To the right,
indigenous houses.

Right-hand page
Flight of stairs
leading from the
spring sanctuary
to the rock
sanctuary.

Before reaching the "Sacred Way", which follows the course of the valley, the itinerary passes an oblong building § of the Hellenistic period (end of 2nd, beginning of 1st century BC) built in large stones (14 x 9 metres). Three columns supported the roof, but only the base of the central column has survived. Its uncertain function was presumably related to the healing sanctuary.

When the cult of the spring had to compete with the civic cults on the forum in Roman times, this building seems to be have been put to agricultural use.

There are two vaulted rooms, each with a fireplace whose brick pillars have been reconstructed. The free smoke evacuation and the large quantities of amphorae found here suggest that it was a smokehouse for preserving wine.

Indigenous Type Houses

Surrounding the smokehouse are houses of simple, indigenous design 9, with only one room, built one above the other against the rock, and served by small sloping alleys. They were left over from the Celto-Ligurian village that preceded the building of the monumental city just before the Roman conquest and were occupied from the 2nd century BC to the 1st century AD. Underneath them, there are earlier traces of habitation from the First Iron Age. In the early Christian period their ruins served as the foundations of new houses.

Acroterion from the roof of the spring showing one of Glanum's mother goddesses with coif, earrings and torque (Gallic necklace). End of 2nd - beginning of 1st century BC.

The Sacred Spring

Following the "Sacred Way" a few metres to the left, opposite the steps, which lead to the rock sanctuary, there is a paved passageway continued by a staircase, leading to the **underground spring** 10. Its therapeutic character gave rise to the water cult, laid the foundation of the settlement and made Glanum prosperous. In the 2nd century BC, an earlier, simple basin, carved in rock, was replaced by the covered building.
The herringbone pattern of the large stone slabs is characteristic of this period (some blocks were replaced at a later stage). The name of the local divinities, the Celtic god Glanis and his beneficent companions, the "Glanic Mothers", are recorded on a large altar (copy) on the opposite side of the street, given as a votive offering by a legionary veteran Marcus Licinius Verecundus in the 1st century AD. A statue of one of the "Glanic Mothers", reproduced in a niche in the wall, has a basket of fruit and a sheaf of corn as symbols of abundance.

to the Celitc god Glanis and the "Glanic Mothers"; the statue of one of them has been placed in a niche. (copies).

Right-hand page (centre)
Altar to Sucellus showing a hand with six fingers and a hammer.

The Healing Water

Sucellus, the hammer god.

Besides the local divinities, Glanis and the "Glanic Mothers", a multitude of healing deities were honoured at Glanum. Among them, Apollo and his Gallic counterpart, Belenos, who were considered to have therapeutic powers by Celts, Greeks and Romans alike. There are about 10 altars, mainly without inscriptions, sometimes with anatomical representations (legs and hands, one has six fingers), which were votive offerings to a divinity that is mostly identified as Sucellus, the hammer god. He was frequently confused with Silvanus — the rural god of the Romans — during the Empire. At Glanum, he seems to have protected the quarrymen in particular.

In Gaul, Mercury, the god of commerce, was often celebrated as a physician in the vicinity of springs. His first representation at Glanum was on a figure capital in the 2nd century BC. There is also a small limestone relief of him with rustic features, naked under his coat, carrying a purse and a wand, dating from Roman times. Fortuna (the Gallic Maia or Rosmerta) stands at his side, holding a horn of plenty and a rudder resting on a globe. A turtle symbolises the celestial arch, and a ram symbolises the fire.

In Roman times, two divinities seemed particularly linked to the water cult and each of them has a monument close to the spring. Hercules is honoured as guardian of the spring, but also as the opener of the passage in the rocky defiles. Valetudo is the Roman goddess of health. Here she seems to reincarnate one of Glanum's beneficial and helpful "Glanic Mothers" of the Celtic tradition.

These healing divinities did not expect valuable offerings from their suppliants and their faithful. The bulk of offerings probably consisted of coins, minuscule stone altars and ex-votos♦ made from wood, as well as food. These did not leave any archaeological traces, but it is likely that they constituted the largest share of offerings, as indicated by the limestone 92cm high, Gallo-Roman statue of a pilgrim who, dressed with a short coat over a tunic, offers the deity a bunch of grapes in gratitude.

Mercury and Fortune

Pilgrim carrying grapes as votive offering.

♦**Ex-votos:** votive offerings.

Two representations of Hercules: in stone *(above)* and in bronze *(below;* Musée Calvet, Avignon).

The Temple of Hercules

Situated to the right of the spring, Hercules' sanctuary was a **modest, square room** measuring 7 metres with a central column. There are no traces of cult activity, but against one of its walls, near the street, Henri Rolland recovered *in situ* **six small altars** (a seventh which had been reused was found subsequently). They surrounded

the base of a statue of Hercules that had fallen to the floor. The 1.30 metre tall statue depicts **Hercules** standing, leaning on his club with the skin of the Nemean lion tied around his neck. In his hand he holds a drinking vessel, evoking the healing water of the spring. The inscription on the base attributes it to lieutenant Gnaeus Pompeius Cornutus who gave the statue as a votive offering in thanks for the healthy return of the tribune Gaius Licinius Macer, and the centurions and soldiers from Glanum who served in the army (2nd century AD). The other altars are also ex-votos.

Dating from the much earlier Hellenistic period is the small, 11 cm high bronze which was found at Saint-Rémy-de-Provence, showing Hercules, naked and beardless. He, too, is carrying a drinking vessel and has a stylised lion skin hanging from his left arm.

The Temple of Valetudo

Situated to the left and dominating the spring, there is a small Corinthian temple 13, partially rebuilt with original fragments: the base, decorated with a frieze; three columns and fragments of a pilaster with its capital. According to the inscription the temple was dedicated to the Roman goddess of health, Valetudo, by Agrippa – Roman general and the son-in-law of the future emperor Augustus – probably during his mission to Gaul in 39 BC.

Opposite, on the other side of the street, there is a small funerary monument 14, dedicated to Gaius Marcius Paetus, which was rebuilt from fragments used in a later wall. The wall's builders probably recovered them from the nearby necropolis.

At the rear the **rampart's** façade and merlons; to the left, **Doric portico.**

The Rampart

Immediately beyond, on the left-hand side, there are the remains of the massive dry-stone Iron Age rampart 15. In front one can see restoration work using large stone slabs from the end of the 2nd and the early 1st century BC. The vehicle gate 16, along the axis of the street, was complemented by a zigzag gate for pedestrians and a small square tower. The walls were crowned with a series of crenellations (merlons) with rounded tops and gargoyles. Underneath the wall there was a sewer; the large flagstones covering it can be seen all along the main street.

The Hellenistic and Roman Monumental Centre

Beyond the vehicle gate there is a large triangular plaza [17]. This must have been the *agora* (public square and market) of the Hellenistic city, since it was surrounded by numerous public monuments. Today the most visible monuments are those that were constructed or rebuilt in Roman times.

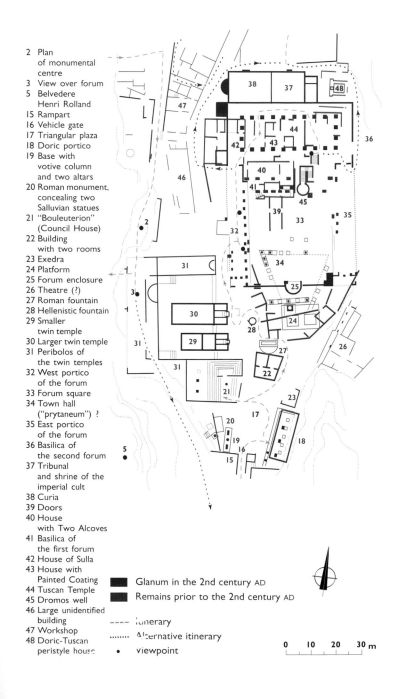

Glanum in the 2nd century AD

Remains prior to the 2nd century AD

---- Itinerary

.... Alternative itinerary

• viewpoint

0   10   20   30 m

The Doric Portico

To the right (east), an elongated portico in the Doric order♦ [18] leans against the rock; part of the **podium** and the **columns** have been preserved (c. 50-25 BC). Three interior columns supported the roof. Beneath this level, one can still see the remains of an even earlier monument, dating to the 2nd and 1st centuries BC. It also was elongated, but had five axial columns and a closed façade. Water conduits in the wall at the bottom fed the small water basins, suggesting that this building, situated at the entrance to the sanctuary, was used for the purification of the worshippers.

Opposite the Doric portico, to the left (west), there are two contemporary buildings. First, an elongated base [19] with a **votive column and two altars.** Just

behind there is another **monument** [20], **decorated with ornamental foliage,** from which a Corinthian capital has been preserved. The statues of **two Celtic dignitaries** sitting cross-legged on a tall, painted base dating from the 2nd and 1st centuries BC were buried beneath its pavement. They used to be placed on either side of the staircase leading to the rock sanctuary. They were surrounded by painted stelae with hollowed-out oval recesses for human skulls.

♦**Doric order:**
Architectural system characterised by columns without bases, with flat grooves, moulded capitals and a frieze with metopes (plain or decorated slabs) and triglyphs (jutting out slabs with vertical grooves).

Hellenistic Buildings next to Roman Monuments

"Bouleuterion"

The so-called *bouleuterion* [21] is located behind the portico. In the Hellenistic city (2nd-1st centuries BC), this was the assembly hall of the local dignitaries. It was an open-air auditorium, surrounded by steps on three sides, and included an altar at the centre; and at the back (west side) a large portico with three axial columns. In Roman times, the northern part was cut off by the construction of the *peribolos* of the "twin temples", but a part of the original wall, made from small stones, and the seating steps are still visible. Before the construction of the basilica, the *bouleuterion* probably served as the *curia* of the Roman town.

Monumental Building with Two Rooms

At the northern end of the Hellenistic *agora* was a building [22] made of large stone slabs, with two rooms opening onto a vestibule. Its vicinity to the *bouleuterion* means it could have been an **administrative building**, perhaps the city archive or treasury.

Exedra

To the east there is a 2nd century BC *exedra* [23], a rectangular niche with benches, which continued to be used in Roman times. On one of its walls, a man called Venustus cut a boat and an architectural landscape (today removed). Some Hellenistic buildings continued to be used in the Roman period, while others (blue on the plan) were demolished and buried under later constructions.

Platform

Following the itinerary to the north, there is a large platform [24]. Dating from Roman times (beginning of the 1st century AD), it is the base of an unidentified monument, which covered a well and basins from an earlier date. Beyond, the visitor can see the enclosure of the forum with its large stone slabs [25] and the semi-circular *exedra* along the axis (end 1st-beginning 2nd century AD).

The Satyr Marsyas

The enclosure of the forum was decorated with representations of the tortured satyr Marsyas, hanging from a tree and skinned alive in punishment for having defied Apollo. Dating to a period shortly after the uprisings that followed Nero's death, one could interpret this as an allusion to the destiny of the rebel cities.

Roman and Hellenistic Fountains

Situated between the tiled platform and the "Monumental Building with Two Rooms", there is a **Roman fountain** [27] with an oblong basin and a semi-circular apse dating to the end of the 1st century BC. Decorated with a miniaturised Corinthian order, it held a statue, which is today lost, and had bas-relief sculptures containing obvious triumphal symbolism, such as Gallic prisoners kneeling on the floor and trophies. Nearby there is a **small circular monument** [28] of the Hellenistic period, made of large stone slabs, which was probably a fountain too.

The Heart of the City,
Four Successive Building Phases
2nd century BC–3rd century AD

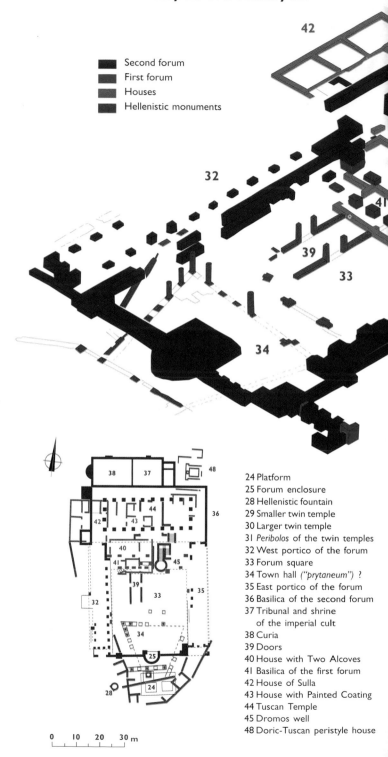

Legend:
- Second forum
- First forum
- Houses
- Hellenistic monuments

42

32

41

39

33

34

38 37

48

36

44

42 43

40

45

41

39

35

32

33

34

25

28 24

0 10 20 30 m

24 Platform
25 Forum enclosure
28 Hellenistic fountain
29 Smaller twin temple
30 Larger twin temple
31 *Peribolos* of the twin temples
32 West portico of the forum
33 Forum square
34 Town hall *("prytaneum")* ?
35 East portico of the forum
36 Basilica of the second forum
37 Tribunal and shrine
   of the imperial cult
38 Curia
39 Doors
40 House with Two Alcoves
41 Basilica of the first forum
42 House of Sulla
43 House with Painted Coating
44 Tuscan Temple
45 Dromos well
48 Doric-Tuscan peristyle house

38

37

43

44

40

36

45

```
0          10          20 m
```

35

One leaves behind (to the left) the (reconstructed) façade of the small twin temple 29 and the foundations of the larger temple 30, in whose foundations the remains of a 1st century BC house are visible. The path leads through the narrow gap between the northern section of the *peribolos* and the western side of the forum. To the right is the west portico of the forum 32, whose façade is marked by a line of square plinths that carried the colonnade. Through the portico, remains of the plaza's paved floor become visible 33, surrounded by the gutter that collected the water from the portico's roof.

Elsewhere, the disappearance of the paving stones has permitted deep excavations, uncovering quite interesting remains from the 2nd and 1st centuries BC. The central valley of Glanum had a regular slope towards the north. When the forum was constructed in the Roman period, the area had to be filled in order to provide a horizontal surface; it was supported further downstream by the walls of the basilica. This work helped to preserve the remains of previous building phases.

There have been four big building programmes on this site, today they are all visible simultaneously and hence cause difficulties in their interpretation.
The Hellenistic monuments (2nd century BC–beginning of the 1st century BC) were replaced by residential houses (c. 90-30 BC). They in turn were buried under the first forum (last quarter of the 1st century BC.), which preceded the second forum whose remains are currently best visible (middle of the 1st century AD–3rd century AD).

Hellenistic Town Hall?

Model of the town centre at the end of the 2nd century BC. In the foreground, is the large trapezoidal shaped building, possibly a town hall. In the centre, a Tuscan order temple surrounded by a *peribolos* and a well with *dromos;* at the back, residential houses

Advancing from south to north, the visitor can recognise, near the southern enclosure of the forum to the right, two columns, a number of bases and a paved floor forming a sharp angle 34. This is the north-west corner of a large trapezoidal shaped Hellenistic building. In the context of the Celto-Ligurian city this could have been the equivalent of a Greek *prytaneum,* the seat of the city's governing body responsible for its political and religious functions. Several aspects support this identification. First the building's location at the edge of the *agora* and in the vicinity of the *bouleuterion,* second, its design: a vast house containing luxurious mosaic pavements, wall decor (terracotta) and the figured capitals of the peristyle courtyard. Third, the contents, especially the drinking vessels and the cult activities, such as the exhibition of human skulls.

The portico, which surrounded the courtyard of the trapezoid building, was decorated with four-headed capitals. The excavations have revealed eight of these intact as well as many fragments. This type of capital originates in Southern Italy, Sicily and Etruria, but these are the work of indigenous artists as can be

Four-headed capital

Cyclops
(top),
Africa
(centre, left),
Female face
(centre, right)
and **male face**
(bottom).

seen by the numerous parallels with the sculptures from the Salluvian *oppidum* Entremont (which preceded the Roman colony of *Aquae Sextiae*). One can recognise the faces of men and women, divinities and heroes, some Graeco-Roman, others Celto-Ligurian, some can be identified by their attributes, others cannot. An allegorical **Africa** is symbolised by an elephant,

Apollo by his laurel crown, Pan by his horns, Mercury by his small, frontal wing, and there is also the one-eyed **Cyclops.** But many of the male and female portraits, some wearing Gallic torques, remain anonymous.

Although the order and sense of these representations escape modern understanding, they are an important testimony to the religious syncretism of the Salluvii.

Under the Julio-Claudian Forum... mid 1st–mid 3rd century AD

From the middle of the forum's west portico, it is relatively easily to recognise the **design of the second Roman forum** if one ignores the ruins, which were buried underneath the plaza's paved floor. There is the square 33 with its two porticos 32, 35, the basilica 36 and its two attachments, the courthouse and the shrine for the imperial cult 37, as well as the *curia* 38. This is the classical plan of a forum for a small provincial city, which was in use between the middle of the 1st to the middle of the 3rd century AD.

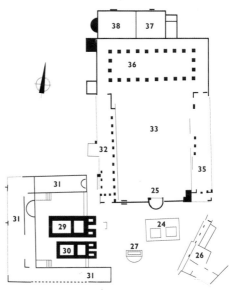

0   10   20   30 m

21 *"Bouleuterion"* (Council House)
24 Platform
25 Forum enclosure
26 Theatre (?)
27 Roman fountain
29 Smaller twin temple
30 Larger twin temple
31 *Peribolos* of the twin temples

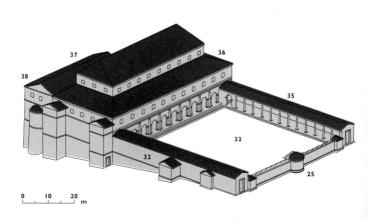

0   10   20 m

But beneath are the remains of a much earlier forum, built in the 20s BC. One can recognise the vestiges of the basilica 41. It was a simple hall with two naves. Foundations of five of the façade columns, three of the axial columns and the ruins of an earlier house in the centre have also survived. The wall at the end has not survived. The construction of this first forum might have followed shortly after the title of *oppidum Latinum* was granted to Glanum; could the larger, second forum of the 1st century AD be considered a testimony to the grant of colonial status?

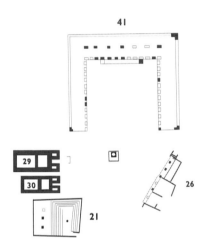

32 West portico of the forum
33 Forum square
35 East portico of the forum
36 Basilica of the second forum
37 Tribunal and shrine of the imperial cult
38 Curia
41 Basilica of the first forum

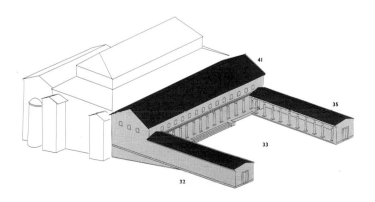

Before leaving the forum's west portico, one should note the two beautiful doors 39 with doorsteps and monolithic jambs. They are the remains of a building joining the Hellenistic *prytaneum* with a monumental well (invisible from here).

40 House
   with Two Alcoves
42 House of Sulla
43 House with
   Painted Coating
45 Dromos well
48 Doric-Tuscan
   peristyle house

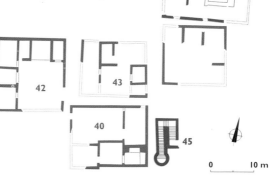

House with Two Alcoves: bedroom with wall painting imitating an architectural order; below, fragment of painted coating (mid 1st century BC). Reconstruction by A. Barbet, F. Trouvé, R. Nunes Pedroso.

House with Two Alcoves

To the left, overlapping with the first basilica, there are the walls of the "house with two alcoves", so-called because its bedroom contains two recesses for beds. Its walls were decorated with the Corinthian architectural order in trompe l'oeil, a fashionable style of the time and well known from Pompeii (middle 1st century BC). The excavations have revealed the short but turbulent history of this house, which was burned down and rebuilt twice in the course of the 1st century BC.

The "house with two alcoves" has two wings around a courtyard without a peristyle. This is a characteristic Mediterranean house type, clearly more comfortable than the indigenous houses seen earlier in the valley of the spring, though less luxurious than the beautiful *domus* in the northern quarter of the city, where similar houses can be found. The house is on a level with the foundations of the second basilica, some 3 metres below its ground floor.

House of Sulla

The House of Sulla 42, cut in
half by the basilica's west wall,
owes its name – probably that
of its owner - to an inscription
on a (removed) mosaic in the
central reception room.

The neighbouring single
bedroom had a pink concrete
floor decorated with cubes of
white marble; its walls were
painted, like those of the
reception room.

**Inscribed
mosaic:**
CO(RNELIVS)
SVLLA.

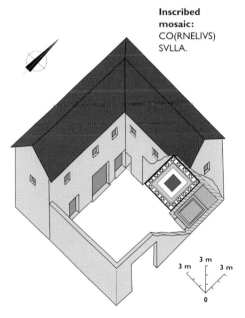

House with
Painted Coating.

Further east are the ruins of
another house 43. One of its
walls has been preserved to a
substantial height and is made
from rejected slab fragments
from the quarry. It still has
traces of red paint coating
on the pink concrete made
of tile fragments.

Other walls, built in quarry
stones, included unbaked
clay bricks.

Model of the Hellenistic monumental centre
(end 2nd-beginning Ist century BC).
To the right, the Tuscan temple; at the centre, the "dromos well"; at the back, the presumed town hall *("prytaneum")*.

The recent discovery
of a well with *dromos (below)* implies that the Tuscan temple was also dedicated to a water cult.

Tuscan Temple

Beneath this house are the demolished foundations of a small Tuscan temple <u>44</u> (2nd century BC-beginning of the Ist century BC). Among the discoveries made here are **blocks from the frieze,** as well as cornices, columns, capitals and plinths decorated with mouldings (exhibited nearby). Without any dedication or traces of any cult activity, it is impossible to identify the divinity that was honoured here, though this temple is closely related to a monument that must have been dedicated to the water cult, the "dromos well" <u>45</u> to the south.

Dromos Well

This well [45], 3 metres in diameter, dates from the late 2nd century BC. Its name derives from the 1.5 metre wide, thrice bent passageway – or *dromos* – with its 37 steps, which leads down to the water level, some 10 metres under the Hellenistic ground level. Originally the entire monument was constructed from large stone slabs, carefully laid out in a "herringbone" pattern. But the casing of the well was dismantled at the beginning of the 1st century BC, like many of Glanum's buildings, and was rebuilt soon after with simple quarry stones like those used for the neighbouring houses. Having been buried under the foundations of the first forum, the well and *dromos* were salvaged in late Antiquity by entrepreneurs who quarried

stones from the abandoned forum. It provided water for the work site, then served as a rubbish pit. Besides heaps of pottery fragments, excavation of the well revealed architectural elements from the forum, such as marble dedications to emperors of the 2nd century AD, statues, and three beautiful **acroteria in the form of theatre masks.**

Right-hand page
**Model
of the northern
district**
in the 2nd century
AD. In the
foreground the
baths: from left
to right, the pool,
the courtyard and
three rooms (two
hot and one cold).
Behind and to the
right, residential
houses.

The Residential District: Baths and Houses

From the "Dromos Well" there are two possible itineraries. The first leads back to the **public baths street,** which was covered by an embankment in antiquity, but excavations have today opened up the sewage canals. To the left, there is the façade of a large, non-identified building 46, next to some utilitarian rooms. To the right, one can recognise the west half of the House of Sulla 42, and the apse of the *curia* made from small stones 38 against which there is an inscribed stele.

The second itinerary goes around the basilica to the east and passes in front of the remains of a house with a Doric-Tuscan peristyle 48.

The two itineraries rejoin behind the imposing buttress walls of the courthouse and *curia* 37, 38.

Net mosaic
(above) **and
Capricorn
mosaic** *(right).*

In the much altered house to the left 49, there were **two mosaics** (today removed). One of them has a motif in waves showing the anterior part of a Capricorn, cantoned by four dolphins, in a diamond shape. The other represents a circular net surrounded by dolphins (first half of the 1st century BC).

Public Baths

In Antiquity public baths had a privileged position in the population's social life and were an important element of "Romanisation". Glanum's baths were built around the third quarter of the 1st century BC and modernised at the end of the 1st century AD. Traces of the earlier design are still visible on the ground, and the earlier swimming pool was partially revealed by the excavations. A beautiful **theatre-mask** of a bearded old man (copy) fed the pool in the second phase 50. Porticoes surrounded the open-air exercise ground, the *palaestra* 51 on three sides; it also had two stone benches. The baths follow a simple, classical layout. Despite the small dimension, the baths included, from right to left, a cold room 52, decorated with half back-to-back columns, two rooms with underground heating (restored brick pillars) and hearths 53, 54; the one on the left 54 had a tub built in the niche of its west wall.

Hellenistic Market

Altar set up by Loreia.

Returning to the main street via the entrance hall of the baths, opposite there is a large door leading to a small Hellenistic market hall built in ashlars 55. It is a courtyard surrounded by Doric columns – one of them has been reconstructed, while only the square plinths of the others have survived. Along its western side there are four shops. In Roman times this courtyard was divided in two by a wall. The southern half 56,

covered and decorated with a bench, was consecrated to the cult of Bona Dea – goddess of the oracle and assimilated to Cybele – as attested by dedications to the religious college of the *dendrophoroi* of Glanum.

There is a **beautiful altar** which was dedicated "to the ears" of a crowned goddess by her priestess Loreia, suggesting a deity who listens to prayers.

Marble relief from the House of Atys.
Lying between a cypress and a pine tree, Cybele's castrated lover is depicted with a shepherd's crook, Phrygian cap and, to the left, panpipes.

House of Atys

The House of Atys 57 takes its name from a representation of **Cybele's lover** on a marble relief that was found here. Its rooms are arranged around an *impluvium* – a small and shallow basin cantoned by four columns whose plinths are still preserved. The well, the benches and the quality of the doorsteps testify to the lavishness of the house: in the Roman period it seems to have served as *schola*, the base for the activities of

the college of *dendrophoroi*. There are numerous altars and an *exedra* with two (restored) columns which probably sheltered a cult. Like the market and the other houses of this quarter, the House of Atys was built in the 2nd century BC (its walls are made of ashlars). All these buildings, however, were in use until the middle of the 3rd century AD, with some more or less significant restorations and changes.

House of the Antae

Leave the House of Atys either by a set of passageways on the south side or retrace the route and enter the House of the Antae <u>58</u>. This is a characteristic example of a Hellenistic Mediterranean house. Its rooms are distributed in three wings around a courtyard with basin surrounded by porticoes (seven Tuscan columns survive). The remains of a flight of stairs signify that there was once an upper storey. The house also included a kitchen and latrines, a large hall facing south and bedrooms. On the west side, an *exedra* was framed by two **antae** (or pillars at the extremity of the wall), decorated with Corinthian capitals.

Returning to the main street, the visitor can see, to the right, the service rooms of the public baths <u>59</u>, with the entrance to the fumaces. On both sides of the street there are the vestiges

of two courtyard houses – the House of Epona <u>60</u> and the house with a simple portico <u>61</u> – that bring the visit to an end.

Cross-section of the reconstructed House of the Antae. At the centre, the hall with the antae, surrounded by bedrooms; to the right, a parlour; to the left, a staircase that leads to the road at the back and to the upper floor.

0   5 m

S   N

The **"Hôtel de Sade"** was built in the 15th century by the Sade, rich dyers from Avignon. It replaced a 14th-century manor house, one of whose walls is still preserved in the courtyard.

The archaeological finds from Glanum are preserved in the "Hôtel de Sade" museum in Saint-Rémy-de-Provence. It is a remarkable collection of architectural and figurative sculpture from Gallo-Greek and Gallo-Roman times. There are inscriptions, paintings, jewellery, pottery, metal objects, etc. which document the private and public tastes, fashions, traditions, customs and beliefs of the people of Glanum.

From top to bottom and from left to right:
Rock crystal ring (1st century AD).
Roman Lamps. Female face
(2nd century BC). **Marble Priapus,**
Roman era. **Altar decorated with**
a garland and a bull's head
(1st century BC).

Pillar with chamber for exhibiting a
skull (2nd-1st centuries BC).
Relief of Diana, the huntress,
Gallo-Roman era.
Altar of the Glanic Dendrophoroi,
Gallo-Roman era.

64 | Selected bibliography

Agusta-Boularot (Sandrine) et Paillet (Jean-Louis), « Le barrage et l'aqueduc occidental de Glanum : le premier barrage-voûte de l'histoire des techniques ? », *Revue Archéologique,* I, 1997, p. 27-78.

Collective, « Glanum, cité grecque et romaine en Provence. Les Antiques », *Les Dossiers d'archéologie,* n° 140, July-August 1989.

Gros (Pierre), « Note sur deux reliefs des « Antiques » de Glanum : le problème de la romanisation », *Revue Archéologique de Narbonnaise,* n° 14, 1981, p. 159-172.

Id., « Le mausolée des Iulii et le statut de Glanum », *Revue Archéologique,* 1986, I, p. 65-80.

Rolland (Henri), *Fouilles de Glanum (Saint-Rémy-de-Provence),* Paris, CNRS, supplément à *Gallia,* n° I, 1946.

Id., *Fouilles de Glanum (1947-1956),* Paris, CNRS, supplement to *Gallia,* n° II, 1958.

Id., *Le Mausolée de Glanum (Saint-Rémy-de-Provence),* Paris, CNRS, supplement to *Gallia,* n° 21, 1969.

Id., *L'Arc de Glanum (Saint-Rémy-de-Provence),* Paris, CNRS, supplement to *Gallia,* n° 31, 1977.

Roth Congès (Anne), « Nouvelles fouilles à Glanum (1982-1990) », *Journal of Roman Archaeology,* n° 5, 1992, p. 39-55.

Id., « La fortune éphémère de Glanum : du religieux à l'économie », *Gallia,* n° 54, 1997, p. 157-202.

Captions

CMN: Centre des monuments nationaux, Paris, formerly Caisse nationale des monuments historiques et des sites.
MAP, AP: Médiathèque de l'architecture et du patrimoine, Archives photographiques, Paris.

Cover
Front: Mont Gaussier dominates the town.
Back: Portrait of an imperial princess.
1st flap: Soffit of the Lares altar in the house of the Antes (detail).
2nd flap
Aerial view.

Visit, page 20: Base of the mausoleum, detail of the relief on the west side.

Chronology
From left to right and from top to bottom.
•Rome: symbol of Rome's foundation: the wolf (5th century BC) feeding Romulus and Remus (added in the 15th century).
Rome, Capitoline Museum, Cl. Malécot collection.
Barbarian fighting a Roman legionary. Paris, Musée du Louvre, RMN/R.-G. Ojeda.
Julius Caesar. Paris, Musée du Louvre, RMN/Chuzeville.
Augustus. Paris, Musée du Louvre, RMN/H. Lewandowski.
Marcus Aurelius and Constantine. Paris, Musée du Louvre, MAP, AP/CNM.
•South-east Gaul: Celto-Ligurian double-head, 5th ?-3rd century BC, Roquepertuse Sanctuary Marseilles, Museum of Archaeology/P. Baguzi.
Agrippa, Paris, Musée du Louvre, RMN/Chuzeville.
Tropaeum Augusti at La Turbie and the amphitheatre in Arles, CNM/A. Lonchampt.
Detail of a sarcophagus, end of 4th century, Arles, Museum of Christian Art.
A. Allemand, Cl. Malécot collection.
•Glanum: Major Events:
Statue of the captured Gaul, CNRS/ Centre Camille Jullian, Aix-en-Provence.
Gaulish prisoner and weapons, CNM/D. Bordes.
•Glanum: public architecture Spring, CNM/D. Bordes.
Mask gargoyle at the baths pool, CNM/D. Bordes.
Small twin temple (reconstruction), CNM/D. Bordes.
Arch, CNM/D. Bordes.
Hercules, CNM/D. Bordes.
•Glanum, private architecture:
House of the Antes, CNM/D. Bordes.
Reconstruction of the bedroom of the house with two alcoves, APPA.
Mausoleum, E.Carraud.
Wine smokery, A. Roth Congès

Maps and Plans
A. Roth Congès: 7, 12b;
A. Roth Congès after IRAA/CNRS: 1st inner flap, 44, 48, 52t-53t;
A. Roth Congès/M. Bouiron after IRAA/CNRS: 54c;
A. Roth Congès after J.-P. Dufoix: 49.

Reconstructions and Models
IRAA-CNRS/F. and F. Trouvé: 32t; A. Roth Congès: 50, 52b-53b; 55b, 61b; A. Roth Congès/F. and F. Trouvé: 56t.

Photograph Credits
Association Pro Pictura Antiqua: 54t; BnF: 11t, 16-17; E. Carraud 13t and c, 20, 22-25; CNM/Ph. Berthé: 21b, 26b, 34, 38; CNM/D. Bordes: 1, 4, 5, 9t and b, 10t, 26t, 27tl and b, 29t, 32b, 33t and br, 35t, 36-37t, 39t and br, 40b, 41, 42t and c, 43, 45ct and cb, 46t, 47tr, 51t and c, 54b, 55b 56c, 58, 59c and br, 60t, c and br, 61, 62, 63 except br; CNM/D. Chenot: front cover, 12t, 35b; CNRS/Centre Camille-Jullian/Aix-en-Provence: back cover, 8, 9c, 10b, 11b, 13b, 21t, 27tr, 30-31, 32t, 39bl, 43b, 45t, cl and b, 50, 51b, 55t, 56t, 57t, 59t, 60bl; L. Damelet/Clic antique: 28, 29b, 40t, 46b, 47 tl, 63br; reproduction L. Damelet/Clic antique: 18, 19t; M. Heller: 2nd outer flap; Cl. Malécot
1st outer flap 33bl, 37b; RMN: 2-3; Ph. Riffaud: 57b; A. Roth Congès: 14, 15, 19b, 36b, 56b, 57t; service régional de l'Archéologie/ PACA/Chr. Hussy: 6t.

Coordinating editor
Alix Sallé

Documentation coordinator
Claude Malécot

Copy editor
Caroline Sunderland
and **Ann Sautier-Greening**

Translator
Ralph Haüssler

Production coordinator
Carine Merse

Design
Atalante/Paris

Layout
encore/Paris

Photoengraving
**Scann'Ouest/
La Chapelle-sur-Erdre**

Printing
**Phénix Impressions/
Bagneux**